"ONCE A BLUE, ALWAYS A BLUE"

For all Evertonians, in the words of their players, managers and the fans who know their history

Designed & edited by Mark Currie

CATΔPULT BOOKS

Official Everton Football Club publication

First Published in 2011 by Catapult Books

First Edition

Copyright © 2011 Catapult Books.
Photographs by kind permission of Everton FC,
Getty Images, Action Images & Liverpool Echo.

Published by Catapult Books

www.catapultbooks.co.uk/sports

ISBN: 978-0-9568581-1-5

A CIP Catalogue of this book is available from
the British Library

Distributed by:
Central Books Ltd
99 Wallis Road
London E9 5LN

Printed and bound in Great Britain by:
Riasca Paper & Print
113 Lidget Street, Lindley, Huddersfield,
West Yorkshire HD3 3JR

"Everton are the people's club in Liverpool. The people on the street support Everton and we hope over the next few years to give them something to be proud of."

David Moyes on the day he joined Everton

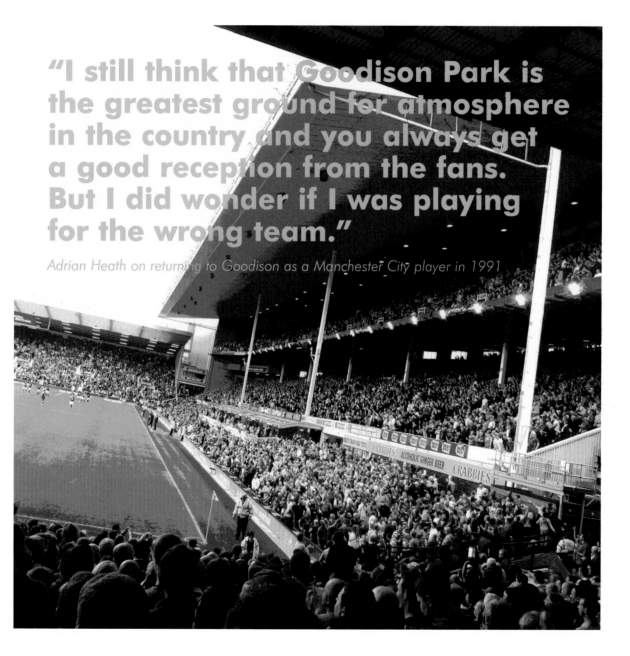

"I still think that Goodison Park is the greatest ground for atmosphere in the country and you always get a good reception from the fans. But I did wonder if I was playing for the wrong team."

Adrian Heath on returning to Goodison as a Manchester City player in 1991

"It was the best 10 years of my career, in fact they are the only team I ever actually played for. That's what happens when you play for Everton, you forget the rest, the rest means nothing."

Duncan Ferguson

"Never forget lads, one Evertonian is worth twenty Liverpudlians."

Brian Labone

"I had one choice to make and I didn't make a mistake. It is a big club with big support."

'King' Louis Saha, scorer of the fastest goal in FA Cup Final history (25 seconds against Chelsea in 2009), on his decision to join Everton a year earlier

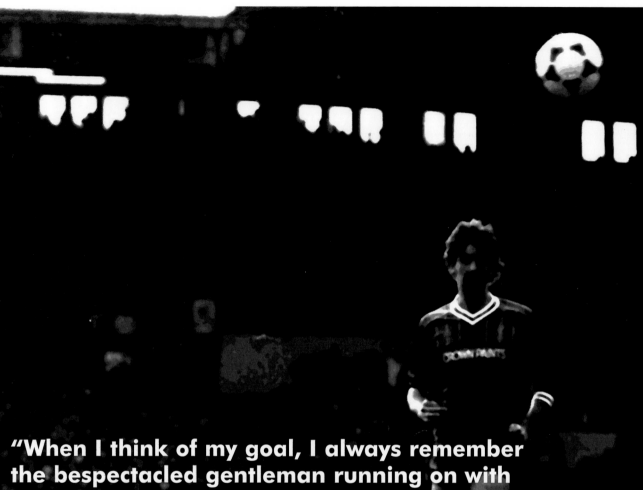

"When I think of my goal, I always remember the bespectacled gentleman running on with the duffle coat and say he's certainly second to Eddie Cavanagh in Everton folklore."

Graeme Sharp on a fan known as 'the Windmill' who invaded the pitch at Anfield in celebration of Sharp's screaming volley that won the derby in 1984

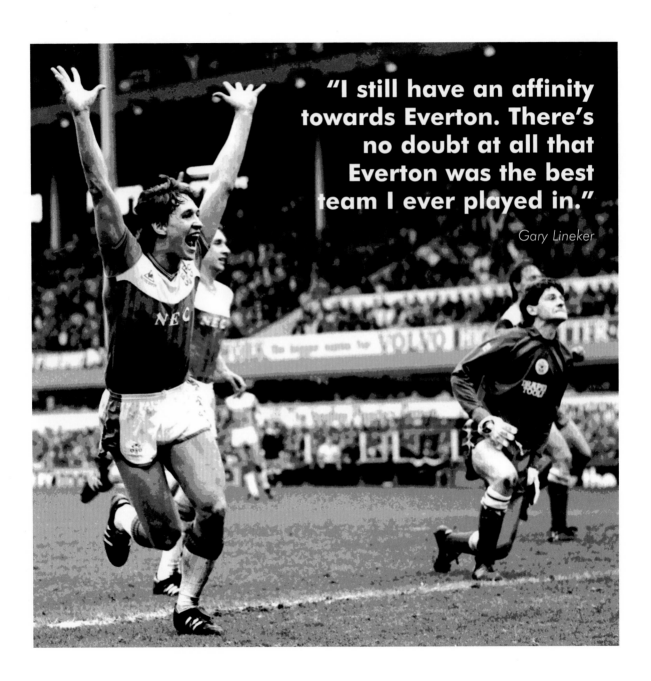

"I still have an affinity towards Everton. There's no doubt at all that Everton was the best team I ever played in."

Gary Lineker

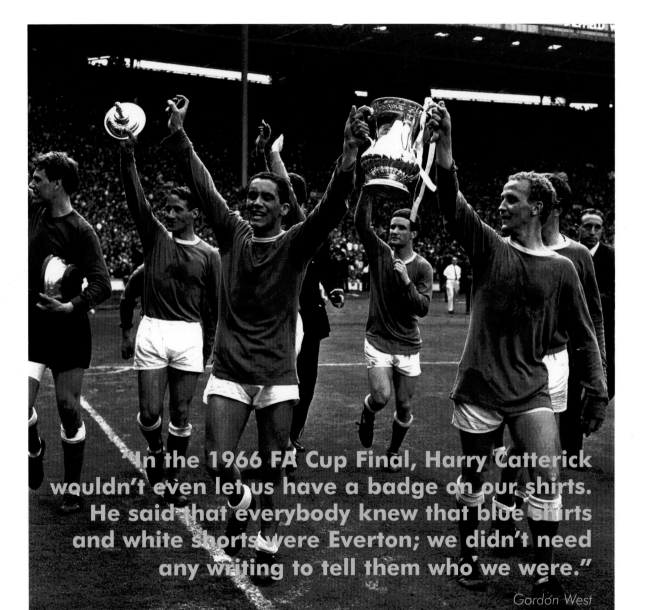

"In the 1966 FA Cup Final, Harry Catterick wouldn't even let us have a badge on our shirts. He said that everybody knew that blue shirts and white shorts were Everton; we didn't need any writing to tell them who we were."

Gordon West

"That's your team-talk. Don't let those fans down."

Howard Kendall, before a make-or-break FA Cup tie at Stoke City in 1984. Dispensing with the traditional pre-match pep-talk, he simply opened the dressing room window to allow his players to hear 10,000 travelling supporters singing. Everton won the game 2-0 and went on to win the FA Cup in May.

"I made my debut at Goodison against Stoke and was standing in the tunnel waiting to go onto the pitch. Z Cars started playing on the PA and I heard the crowd roar. If I could bottle a moment and save it forever, then that would be it."

Alan Harper

"Dixie was the greatest centre forward there will ever be. His record of goal scoring is the most amazing thing under the sun. He belongs in the company of the supremely great like Beethoven, Shakespeare and Rembrandt."

Bill Shankly on Dixie Dean, who died on 1st March 1980 at Goodison Park, watching the Merseyside derby

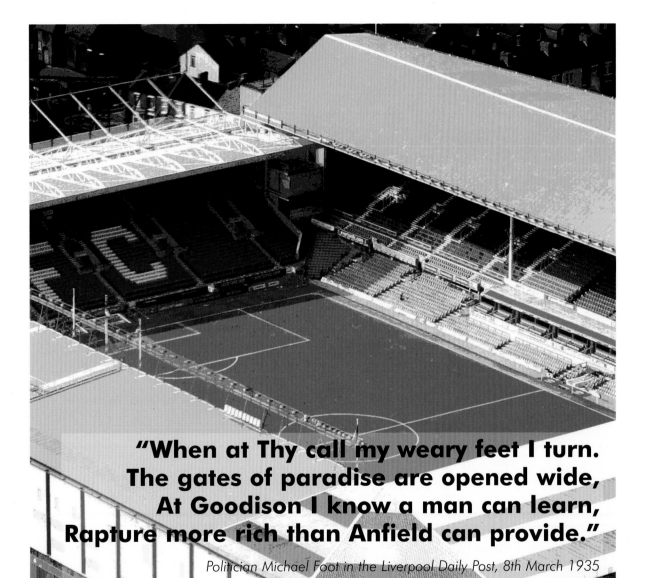

**"When at Thy call my weary feet I turn.
The gates of paradise are opened wide,
At Goodison I know a man can learn,
Rapture more rich than Anfield can provide."**

Politician Michael Foot in the Liverpool Daily Post, 8th March 1935

"I usually just put one finger up signalling a goal, but, it being the Kop end, two fingers automatically went up. I got hauled up in front of the FA and I was like Ted Rogers trying to go from two fingers to one and trying to convince them it wasn't a V-sign."

Kevin Sheedy on scoring against Liverpool at Anfield

"If they're willing to have me, I'll stay as long as they want me. It's an amazing club, and it's a place where I feel like I can compete."

Tim Howard

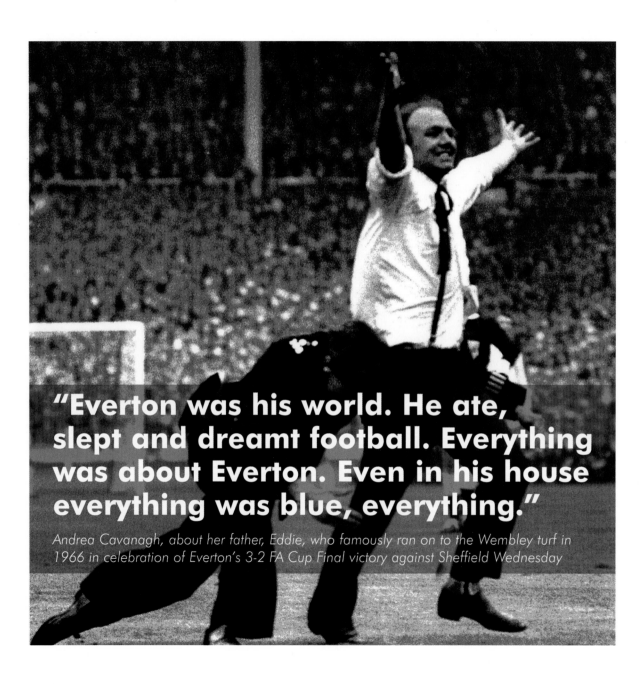

"Everton was his world. He ate, slept and dreamt football. Everything was about Everton. Even in his house everything was blue, everything."

Andrea Cavanagh, about her father, Eddie, who famously ran on to the Wembley turf in 1966 in celebration of Everton's 3-2 FA Cup Final victory against Sheffield Wednesday

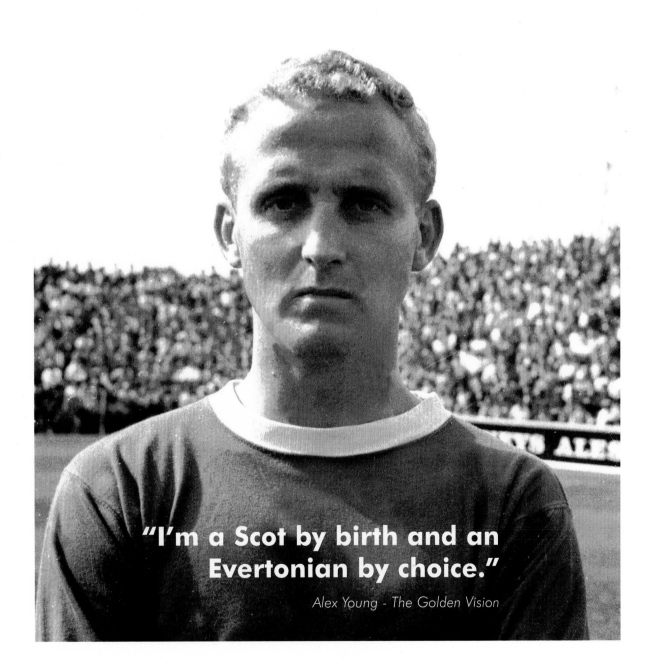

"I'm a Scot by birth and an Evertonian by choice."

Alex Young - The Golden Vision

"I was running back to the centre circle after I scored the second goal against Liverpool and pure elation welled up inside me. I remember thinking, I just love this place - I want this place forever."

Alan Ball, August 1966

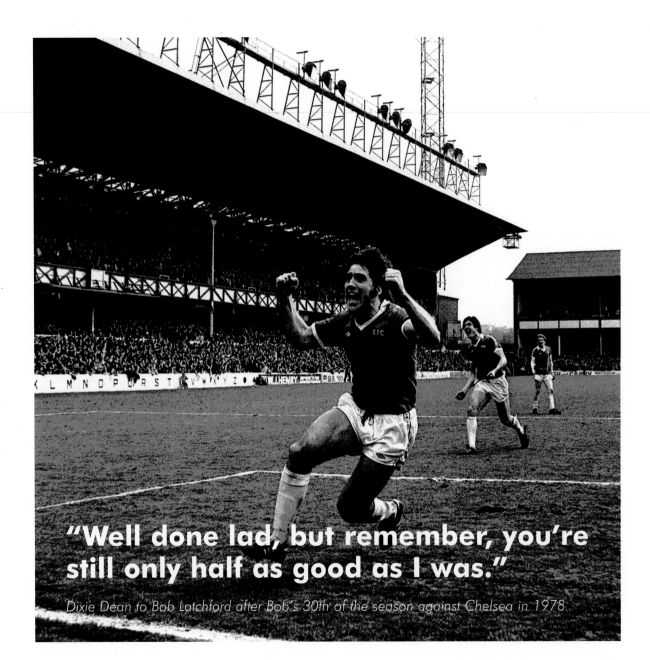

"Well done lad, but remember, you're still only half as good as I was."

Dixie Dean to Bob Latchford after Bob's 30th of the season against Chelsea in 1978

"I was in the crowd when Bob Latchford scored a penalty in the last minute. There was a mass invasion of the pitch and I was one of those who ran on."

Derek Mountfield on Everton's 6-0 win over Chelsea in 1978

"The Evertonians ran on the pitch and put blue scarves on me. I walked towards the fans to thank them and let them know how much I missed them."

Jimmy Gabriel on his return to Goodison Park as a Southampton player in 1968

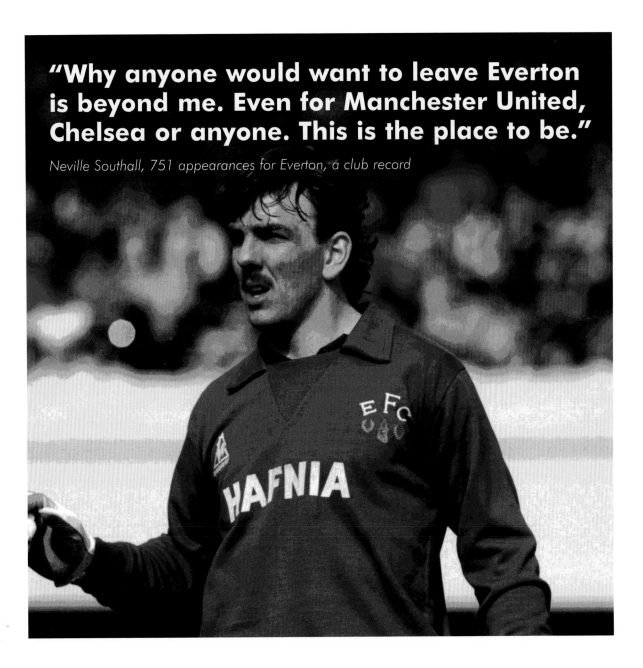

"Why anyone would want to leave Everton is beyond me. Even for Manchester United, Chelsea or anyone. This is the place to be."

Neville Southall, 751 appearances for Everton, a club record

"Everton have always been noted for going out on the pitch to play football. We got called the School of Science quite rightly. The other lot, the Reds...well they were a gang of butchers! They should have been working in an abattoir. McNab, McKinlay, the Wadsworths. God bless my soul. They'd kick an old woman."

Dixie Dean

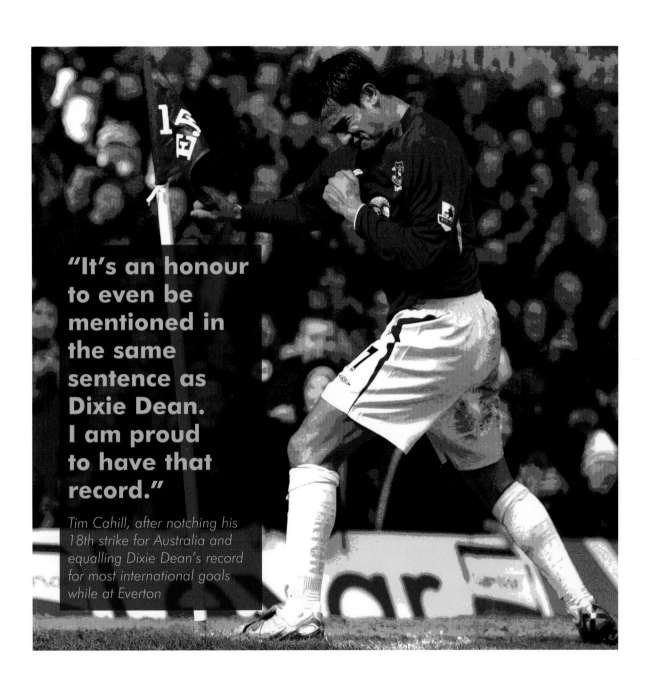

"It's an honour to even be mentioned in the same sentence as Dixie Dean. I am proud to have that record."

Tim Cahill, after notching his 18th strike for Australia and equalling Dixie Dean's record for most international goals while at Everton

"We love Andy Gray so much that, if I found him in bed with my wife, I'd tuck him in and make sure he didn't catch cold!"

Everton fan, Pedro Bishop

"You can have love affairs with other football clubs. With Everton it's a marriage."

Howard Kendall

"I want to win everything, but I want to win it all with Everton."

Jack Rodwell, March 2010

"The best team of the lot was 1969-70. It's no wonder we were champions. That was the best Everton side ever and it's never been bettered to this day."

Gordon West, goalkeeper from 1961 to 1973

"Everton are a bigger club than Liverpool. Everywhere you go on Merseyside you bump into Everton supporters."

Ex Liverpool player, Graeme Souness

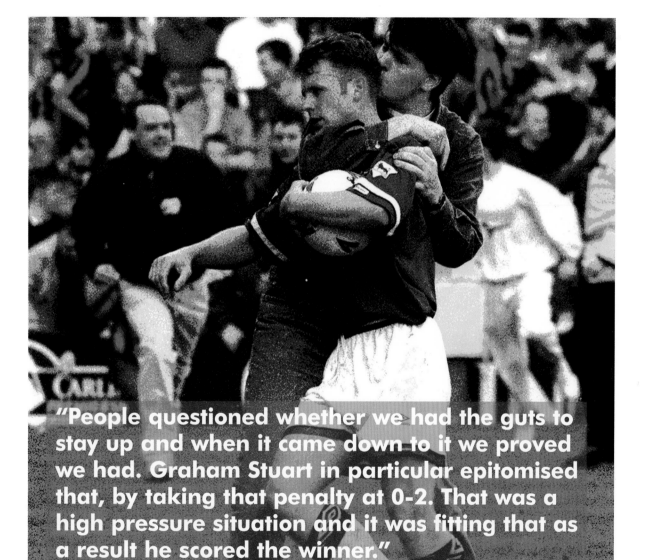

"People questioned whether we had the guts to stay up and when it came down to it we proved we had. Graham Stuart in particular epitomised that, by taking that penalty at 0-2. That was a high pressure situation and it was fitting that as a result he scored the winner."

Mike Walker, after Everton beat Wimbledon 3-2 to avoid relegation, May 1994

"I love playing for Everton. I love the spirit in the club. I love the togetherness."

Phil Neville on signing a new contract, August 2011

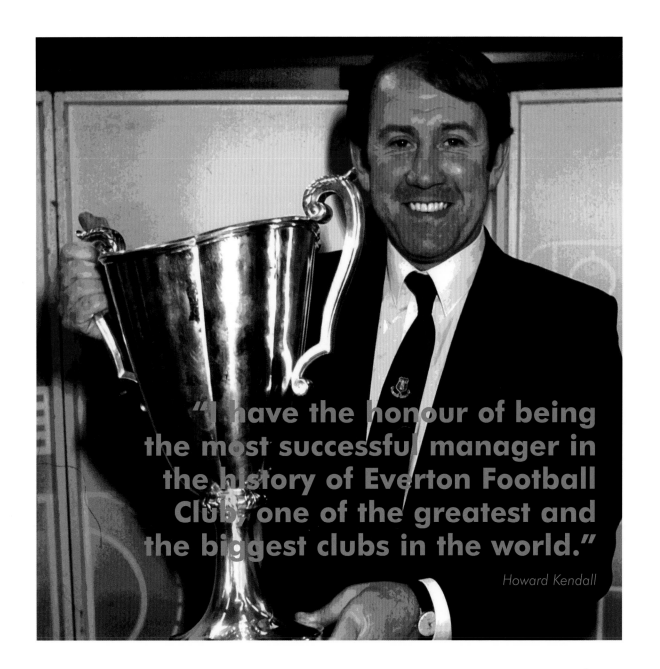

"I have the honour of being the most successful manager in the history of Everton Football Club, one of the greatest and the biggest clubs in the world."

Howard Kendall

"Goodison Park just seems to be a magical place. There was something that made the back of my neck tingle when I ran on to the pitch even when the place was empty."

Alex Young

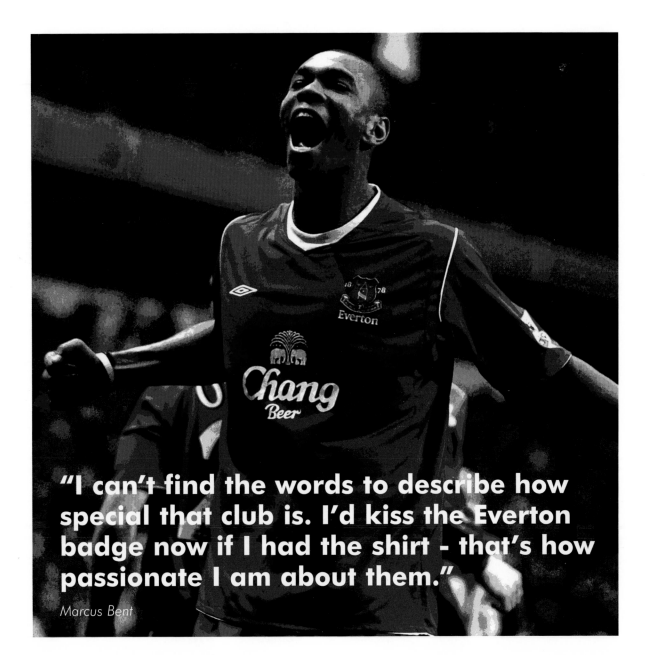

"I can't find the words to describe how special that club is. I'd kiss the Everton badge now if I had the shirt - that's how passionate I am about them."

Marcus Bent

"Everton were just too good for us. It's been a long time since we played against anyone of their class. They are possibly the best side in the whole of Europe."

Hans Krankl, after his side, Rapid Vienna, were beaten in the European Cup Winners' Cup Final, 3-1 by Everton in 1985

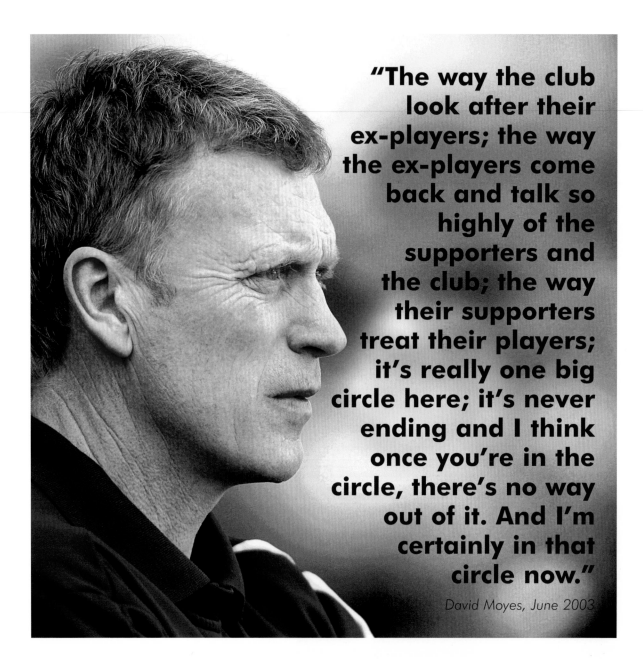

"The way the club look after their ex-players; the way the ex-players come back and talk so highly of the supporters and the club; the way their supporters treat their players; it's really one big circle here; it's never ending and I think once you're in the circle, there's no way out of it. And I'm certainly in that circle now."

David Moyes, June 2003

"I'd never seen anything like it. It was like the whole of Liverpool had turned out to welcome me back."

Duncan McKenzie on his return to Goodison Park as a Chelsea player in 1978

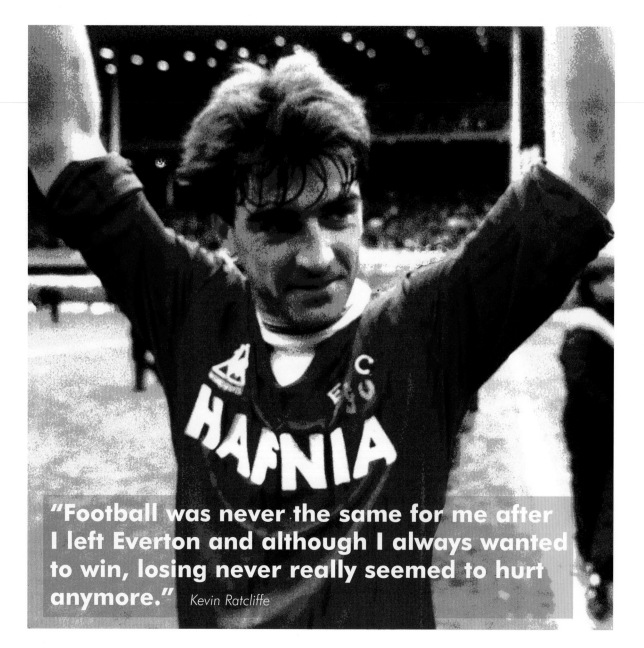

"Football was never the same for me after I left Everton and although I always wanted to win, losing never really seemed to hurt anymore." *Kevin Ratcliffe*

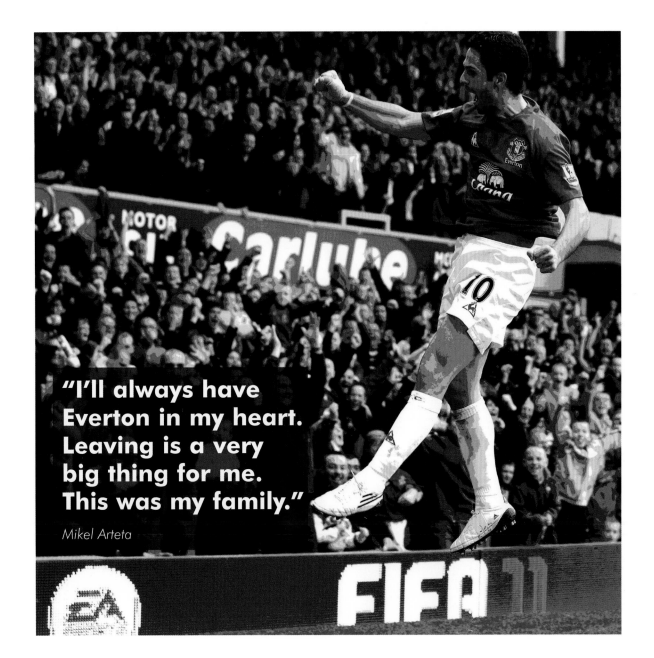

"I'll always have Everton in my heart. Leaving is a very big thing for me. This was my family."

Mikel Arteta

"I would have broken every bone in my body for any other club, but I would have died for Everton."

Dave 'The Cannonball Kid' Hickson

"If they got beat he was awful to live with because he loved Everton so much. He is Everton and Everton is him."

Trisha Lyons on husband Mick's Royal Blue blood

"People ask me if that 60-goal record will ever be beaten. I think it will. But there's only one man who'll do it. That's that feller who walks on the water."

Dixie Dean

"Scoring for Everton was better than sex."

Bob Latchford